The story begins

The tale of creation and fall

Z AP! ZAP! Two spaceships explode.

"Jon!" a voice yells. "Homework!"

"Aw, Mum!" called Jon. "I'm, er, thinking. I've got to write about a great love story – yuk!"

Jon doodled a face on his computer mouse and pulled out his Bible. "There must be a love story in this load of old … stuff!"

"Neep! Neep!" said his mouse. "Yes, Jon. And I am going to help you find one."

"Weird! Hey, come back!"

The mouse vanishes through the screen. Jon grabs the tail and is pulled inside. He whirls through corridors of lights into a room piled with books.

"Mouse!" he shouts. "Oh, sorry!"

"Who are you?" asks Jon.

"I'm the Scribe. I study this load of old …" he coughed, "stuff. Now about that homework."

"Love stories are for wimps!"

"Not this one. Have you heard of 'Shema'? It's Hebrew for listen."

"'Shema' – listen. I'll tell you a love story. But watch out. It has some ugly twists. Well, here we go. And to think I could have stayed in my nice warm study."

"Oh, no! Not again! Help!"

Jon and Storymouse are whisked into the air and sent careering into space, past explosions of light, through aeons of darkness.

"It all started way back when time began. The Earth was a whirling mass of molten metals and gases. It was completely black."

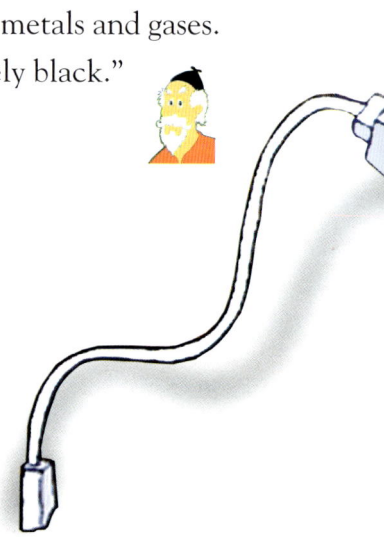

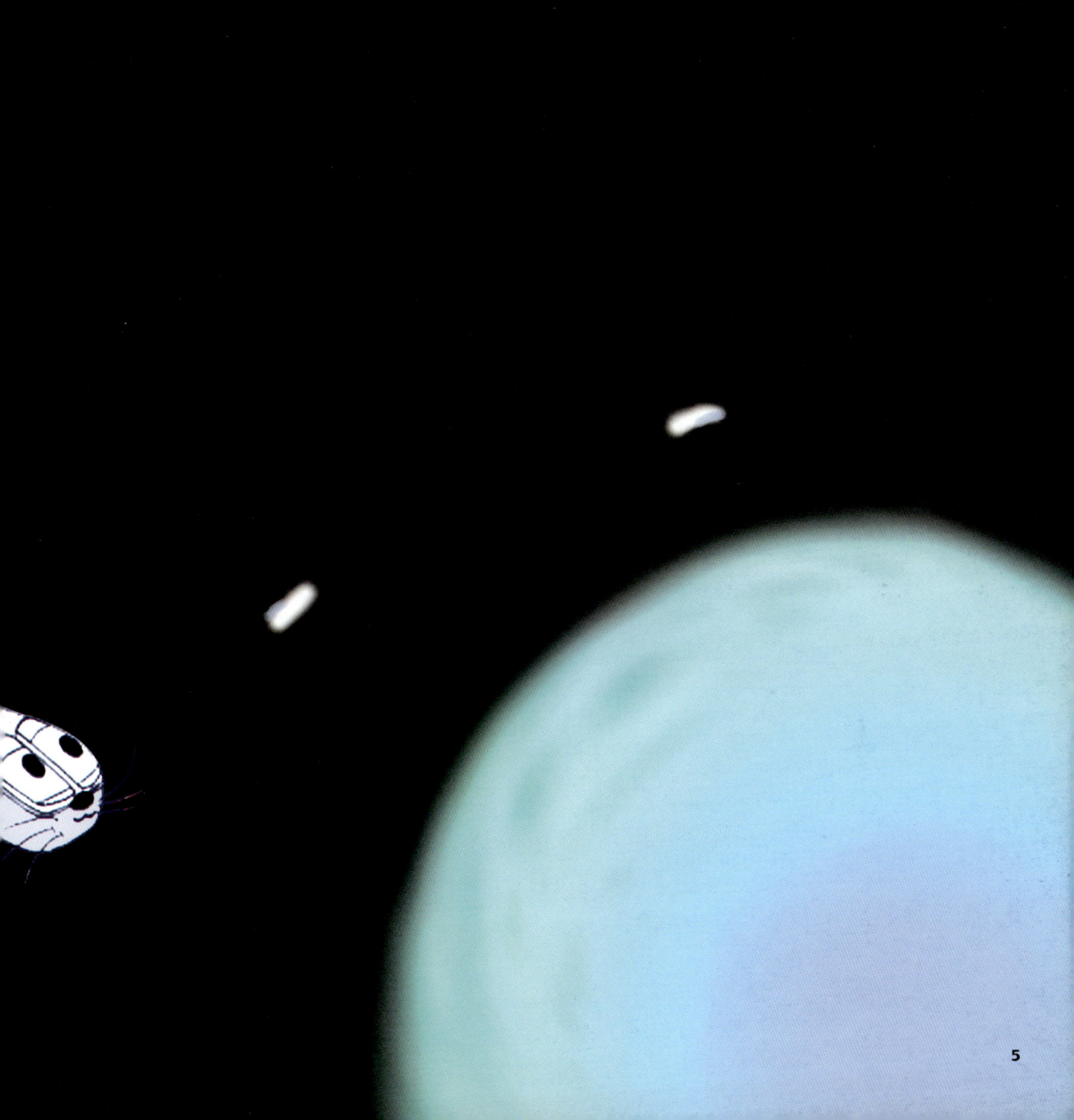

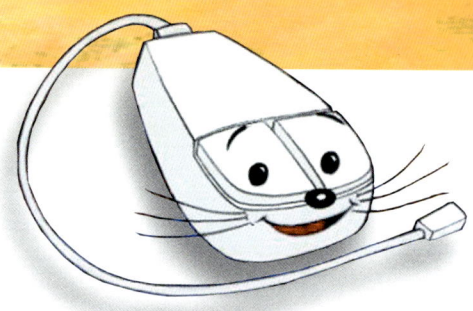

 "Thick blackness was all there was. Then God breathed. God said, 'Let light come.' And light came. That's how it started. In the beginning God made sky and the earth, and then night and day."

 "Whooaoaoh! Touchdown! Ouch!"

"For wimps, is it?"

The Scribe rubbed his knee. He stood up and dusted down his robe.

 "Ahem. Welcome to the Garden of Eden, Jon. The start of your love story. It's the dawning of the world."

"Doesn't look much like a garden to me. It's all dust and rock."

"That's because God is still making his world. You should have seen it yesterday. No dry land anywhere. Shema – listen."

 "I can hear water!"

Jon spins round. A clear stream ripples over pebbles.

"A drink, just what I need."

 "Keep looking."

"Wow!"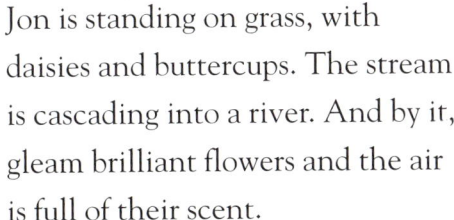

Jon is standing on grass, with daisies and buttercups. The stream is cascading into a river. And by it, gleam brilliant flowers and the air is full of their scent.

"Look! Don't just stare at the ground!"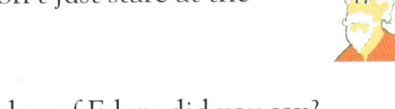

"The Garden of Eden, did you say? It's more like a park. I wouldn't mind exploring. Great!"

Jon races for a tree and hauls himself up on to a branch. He sees hills, and woods and more flowers. And just ahead, a wide lake.

"What's this? Apples! And that tree has oranges. And there's a nut tree. Yummy! I'm starving. I missed my supper!"

"Watch out, mouse! There's a cat! Oh-er! That's not a cat. I'm glad I'm up this tree. You didn't warn me that the garden was dangerous, Scribe."

"Come on down, Jon. Don't be alarmed. God has been making birds, and fish and insects and all kinds of animals. And they're all happy and peaceful together. Listen. Look.

"God is pleased. His world is very good. But something's missing."

"Mr Scribe, who are they?"

"Adam and Eve. Haven't you heard about them?"

"But they've got no clothes on!"

"Well, it's warm in the garden. And besides it never occurred to them to be embarrassed.

"God was very happy when he  made Adam and Eve. 'They're like me,' he said."

"I don't get that, has God got a body?"

"No. But you can be like your Mum, can't you, even though you don't look like her? You often behave like her. She says you've got her temper.

"Well, Adam and Eve can love, and imagine, and make things, most of all, make decisions. They have free will. Just like God. They

aren't robots. God loves Adam and Eve and he wants them to love him. But I must say, he's taking a risk.

"God said to Adam and Eve, 'I'm putting you in charge of the garden. Look after it. And take care of the animals. There's fruit and nuts for you to eat and plants for the animals. Have children and be happy.'

"God talked to Adam and Eve every day and they chat about all they've been doing. At least, they do at first.

"What do you mean, 'at first'?"

"I warned you there were some nasty twists. Well, God says to Adam and Eve, 'You can eat the fruit from every tree except the fruit on the tree of the knowledge of good and evil. If you eat that, you'll die.' That tree is in the middle of the garden, next to the tree with fruit that gives life for ever."

"Creepy! What's that?"

"There's danger in the garden."

"I knew it!"

"No, not from any animal but from an evil angel called Satan. He's disguised himself to look like a serpent, and slides among the trees, waiting his chance."

"Neep."

"One day he slithers up to Eve when she's by herself. 'Can't you eat the fruit on the trees?'

"'Yes, we can,' Eve says. 'We can eat any fruit we want except for the fruit on the tree of the knowledge of good and evil. If we eat that, we'll die.'

"'That's God's story,' hisses the serpent. 'He's selfish. He's keeping the best for himself. You're free to choose, so choose what's best for you. Choose greatness. The truth is, if you eat that fruit you'll be as clever as God. And he doesn't want that.'"

"Eve stares at the fruit. It looks delicious. Her mouth waters She thinks, 'I want to be as clever as God. Why should he stop me?'

"Her hand reaches up."

"Oh, no! Don't!"

"She picks the fruit, and takes a bite. Then another. She gobbles it down.

"Eve waits to see if she's going to die. But nothing happens. So she dashes off to tell Adam. And he eats the fruit, too.

"That evening God calls Adam and Eve as usual."

"If I'd been Adam and Eve, I'd have scarpered. I couldn't have faced him."

"Quite. They hide. But God knows anyway. 'Have you eaten the fruit?' God asks. Adam accuses Eve, and God too. He says, 'The woman you gave me made me eat it.'

"'What have you done?' God asks Eve.

"'It's all the serpent's fault,' she says."

"Now what'll happen? Is that a divorce? Is that the end of the love story? And why didn't they die? Why doesn't God send a flash of lightning and kill them?"

"God didn't send a flash of lightning because he still loves Adam and Eve."

"What's happened to the garden?"

"The wrong they'd done was like a virus. It's infected all creation. There are briars and brambles. Work is hard. Lots of animals have turned bloodthirsty."

"Look, they're going away!"

"Yes, they can no longer eat fruit from the tree that gives life for ever, so they have to leave the Garden. So you see, they will die, but not straight away."

"So is that the end? What a rotten love story."

 "No, that's not the end. It's only the beginning. God still loves Adam and Eve. He makes warm clothes for them out of animal skins. And he makes a promise. One day a Rescuer will come and destroy the power of that dark angel. And God stays with them when they leave the garden.

"Satan hasn't given up either. He's always watching and waiting for a chance to cause more havoc. As you'll soon see.

"But just think, if Adam and Eve had only trusted God, if they'd only believed that he loved them and knew best, then that tragedy would never had happened. But God never forces people to do what's right."

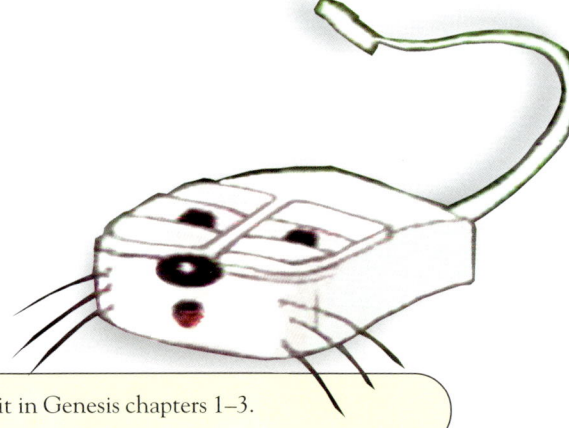

This story is in the Bible. You can find it in Genesis chapters 1–3.